THIS BOOK BELONGS TO:

CONTACT INFORMATION	
NAME:	
ADDRESS:	
PHONE:	

START / END DATES

/ /   TO   / /

PLANNING CALENDAR

JANUARY

FEBRUARY

MARCH

APRIL

MAY

JUNE

PLANNING CALENDAR

JULY

AUGUST

SEPTEMBER

OCTOBER

NOVEMBER

DECEMBER

CALVING RECORD

CALF ID	COW ID	SIRE ID	BIRTH DATE	SEX	CALVING EASE	CALF VIGOR

BIRTH WEIGHT	CALF NURSED (YES /NO)	WEANING WEIGHT	WEANING DATE	COW BCS	NOTES

CALVING RECORD

CALF ID	COW ID	SIRE ID	BIRTH DATE	SEX	CALVING EASE	CALF VIGOR

BIRTH WEIGHT	CALF NURSED (YES /NO)	WEANING WEIGHT	WEANING DATE	COW BCS	NOTES

CALVING RECORD

CALF ID	COW ID	SIRE ID	BIRTH DATE	SEX	CALVING EASE	CALF VIGOR

BIRTH WEIGHT	CALF NURSED (YES /NO)	WEANING WEIGHT	WEANING DATE	COW BCS	NOTES

CALVING RECORD

CALF ID	COW ID	SIRE ID	BIRTH DATE	SEX	CALVING EASE	CALF VIGOR

BIRTH WEIGHT	CALF NURSED (YES /NO)	WEANING WEIGHT	WEANING DATE	COW BCS	NOTES

A.I./BULL BREEDING RECORD

COW ID	DATE	1ST SERVICE	BULL ID	ESTIMATED CALVING DATE

DATE	2ND SERVICE	BULL ID	ESTIMATED CALVING DATE	A.I TECH

A.I./BULL BREEDING RECORD

COW ID	DATE	1ST SERVICE	BULL ID	ESTIMATED CALVING DATE

DATE	2ND SERVICE	BULL ID	ESTIMATED CALVING DATE	A.I TECH

A.I./BULL BREEDING RECORD

COW ID	DATE	1ST SERVICE	BULL ID	ESTIMATED CALVING DATE

DATE	2ND SERVICE	BULL ID	ESTIMATED CALVING DATE	A.I TECH

A.I./BULL BREEDING RECORD

COW ID	DATE	1ST SERVICE	BULL ID	ESTIMATED CALVING DATE

DATE	2ND SERVICE	BULL ID	ESTIMATED CALVING DATE	A.I TECH

COW PRODUCTION HISTORY CARD

COW REGISTRATION #:			
DESCRIPTION (BREED/COLOR)			
COW'S SIRE		SIRE BREED:	
COW'S DAM		DAM BREED	
COW'S BIRTH DATE		WEANING WEIGHT	
PURCHASE DATE		PURCHASE PRICE	

BREEDING RECORD

WEIGHT AT FIRST SERVICE (KGS)				
AGE AT FIRST SERVICE (DAYS)				
HEAT DATES	DATE OF A.I/BULL SERVICE	PREG. DIAGNOSIS DATE	DATE TO DRY	DATE DUE TO CALF

COW ID #	

DATE OF SALE OR REMOVAL:	
REASON	
SALE WEIGHT	
SALE PRICE/LB.	
TOTAL VALUE	

AGE AT FIRST CALVING (DAYS)				
AGE AT CONCEPTION (DAYS)				
DATE CALVED	CALF SEX	CALF NO.	CALVING INTERNAL (DAYS)	NOTES

COW PRODUCTION HISTORY CARD

COW REGISTRATION #:			
DESCRIPTION (BREED/COLOR)			
COW'S SIRE		SIRE BREED:	
COW'S DAM		DAM BREED	
COW'S BIRTH DATE		WEANING WEIGHT	
PURCHASE DATE		PURCHASE PRICE	

BREEDING RECORD

WEIGHT AT FIRST SERVICE (KGS)				
AGE AT FIRST SERVICE (DAYS)				
HEAT DATES	DATE OF A.I/BULL SERVICE	PREG. DIAGNOSIS DATE	DATE TO DRY	DATE DUE TO CALF

COW ID

DATE OF SALE OR REMOVAL:	
REASON	
SALE WEIGHT	
SALE PRICE/LB.	
TOTAL VALUE	

AGE AT FIRST CALVING (DAYS)				
AGE AT CONCEPTION (DAYS)				
DATE CALVED	CALF SEX	CALF NO.	CALVING INTERNAL (DAYS)	NOTES

COW PRODUCTION HISTORY CARD

COW REGISTRATION #:			
DESCRIPTION (BREED/COLOR)			
COW'S SIRE		SIRE BREED:	
COW'S DAM		DAM BREED	
COW'S BIRTH DATE		WEANING WEIGHT	
PURCHASE DATE		PURCHASE PRICE	

BREEDING RECORD

WEIGHT AT FIRST SERVICE (KGS)			
AGE AT FIRST SERVICE (DAYS)			

HEAT DATES	DATE OF A.I/BULL SERVICE	PREG. DIAGNOSIS DATE	DATE TO DRY	DATE DUE TO CALF

COW ID

DATE OF SALE OR REMOVAL:	
REASON	
SALE WEIGHT	
SALE PRICE/LB.	
TOTAL VALUE	

AGE AT FIRST CALVING (DAYS)				
AGE AT CONCEPTION (DAYS)				
DATE CALVED	CALF SEX	CALF NO.	CALVING INTERNAL (DAYS)	NOTES

COW PRODUCTION HISTORY CARD

COW REGISTRATION #:			
DESCRIPTION (BREED/COLOR)			
COW'S SIRE		SIRE BREED:	
COW'S DAM		DAM BREED	
COW'S BIRTH DATE		WEANING WEIGHT	
PURCHASE DATE		PURCHASE PRICE	

BREEDING RECORD

	WEIGHT AT FIRST SERVICE (KGS)			
	AGE AT FIRST SERVICE (DAYS)			
HEAT DATES	DATE OF A.I/BULL SERVICE	PREG. DIAGNOSIS DATE	DATE TO DRY	DATE DUE TO CALF

COW ID

DATE OF SALE OR REMOVAL:	
REASON	
SALE WEIGHT	
SALE PRICE/LB.	
TOTAL VALUE	

	AGE AT FIRST CALVING (DAYS)			
	AGE AT CONCEPTION (DAYS)			
DATE CALVED	CALF SEX	CALF NO.	CALVING INTERNAL (DAYS)	NOTES

COW PRODUCTION HISTORY CARD

COW REGISTRATION #:			
DESCRIPTION (BREED/COLOR)			
COW'S SIRE		SIRE BREED:	
COW'S DAM		DAM BREED	
COW'S BIRTH DATE		WEANING WEIGHT	
PURCHASE DATE		PURCHASE PRICE	

BREEDING RECORD

WEIGHT AT FIRST SERVICE (KGS)				
AGE AT FIRST SERVICE (DAYS)				
HEAT DATES	DATE OF A.I/BULL SERVICE	PREG. DIAGNOSIS DATE	DATE TO DRY	DATE DUE TO CALF

COW ID #	

DATE OF SALE OR REMOVAL:	
REASON	
SALE WEIGHT	
SALE PRICE/LB.	
TOTAL VALUE	

AGE AT FIRST CALVING (DAYS)				
AGE AT CONCEPTION (DAYS)				
DATE CALVED	CALF SEX	CALF NO.	CALVING INTERNAL (DAYS)	NOTES

COW PRODUCTION HISTORY CARD

COW REGISTRATION #:			
DESCRIPTION (BREED/COLOR)			
COW'S SIRE		SIRE BREED:	
COW'S DAM		DAM BREED	
COW'S BIRTH DATE		WEANING WEIGHT	
PURCHASE DATE		PURCHASE PRICE	

BREEDING RECORD

WEIGHT AT FIRST SERVICE (KGS)				
AGE AT FIRST SERVICE (DAYS)				
HEAT DATES	DATE OF A.I/BULL SERVICE	PREG. DIAGNOSIS DATE	DATE TO DRY	DATE DUE TO CALF

COW ID #	

DATE OF SALE OR REMOVAL:	
REASON	
SALE WEIGHT	
SALE PRICE/LB.	
TOTAL VALUE	

	AGE AT FIRST CALVING (DAYS)			
	AGE AT CONCEPTION (DAYS)			
DATE CALVED	CALF SEX	CALF NO.	CALVING INTERNAL (DAYS)	NOTES

COW PRODUCTION HISTORY CARD

COW REGISTRATION #:			
DESCRIPTION (BREED/COLOR)			
COW'S SIRE		SIRE BREED:	
COW'S DAM		DAM BREED	
COW'S BIRTH DATE		WEANING WEIGHT	
PURCHASE DATE		PURCHASE PRICE	

BREEDING RECORD

WEIGHT AT FIRST SERVICE (KGS)				
AGE AT FIRST SERVICE (DAYS)				
HEAT DATES	DATE OF A.I/BULL SERVICE	PREG. DIAGNOSIS DATE	DATE TO DRY	DATE DUE TO CALF

COW ID

DATE OF SALE OR REMOVAL:	
REASON	
SALE WEIGHT	
SALE PRICE/LB.	
TOTAL VALUE	

AGE AT FIRST CALVING (DAYS)				
AGE AT CONCEPTION (DAYS)				
DATE CALVED	CALF SEX	CALF NO.	CALVING INTERNAL (DAYS)	NOTES

COW PRODUCTION HISTORY CARD

COW REGISTRATION #:			
DESCRIPTION (BREED/COLOR)			
COW'S SIRE		SIRE BREED:	
COW'S DAM		DAM BREED	
COW'S BIRTH DATE		WEANING WEIGHT	
PURCHASE DATE		PURCHASE PRICE	

BREEDING RECORD

WEIGHT AT FIRST SERVICE (KGS)				
AGE AT FIRST SERVICE (DAYS)				
HEAT DATES	DATE OF A.I/BULL SERVICE	PREG. DIAGNOSIS DATE	DATE TO DRY	DATE DUE TO CALF

COW ID #	

DATE OF SALE OR REMOVAL:	
REASON	
SALE WEIGHT	
SALE PRICE/LB.	
TOTAL VALUE	

	AGE AT FIRST CALVING (DAYS)			
	AGE AT CONCEPTION (DAYS)			
DATE CALVED	CALF SEX	CALF NO.	CALVING INTERNAL (DAYS)	NOTES

COW PRODUCTION HISTORY CARD

COW REGISTRATION #:

DESCRIPTION (BREED/COLOR)

COW'S SIRE		SIRE BREED:	
COW'S DAM		DAM BREED	
COW'S BIRTH DATE		WEANING WEIGHT	
PURCHASE DATE		PURCHASE PRICE	

BREEDING RECORD

WEIGHT AT FIRST SERVICE (KGS)				
AGE AT FIRST SERVICE (DAYS)				
HEAT DATES	DATE OF A.I/BULL SERVICE	PREG. DIAGNOSIS DATE	DATE TO DRY	DATE DUE TO CALF

COW ID #	

DATE OF SALE OR REMOVAL:	
REASON	
SALE WEIGHT	
SALE PRICE/LB.	
TOTAL VALUE	

AGE AT FIRST CALVING (DAYS)					
AGE AT CONCEPTION (DAYS)					
DATE CALVED	CALF SEX	CALF NO.	CALVING INTERNAL (DAYS)		NOTES

COW PRODUCTION HISTORY CARD

COW REGISTRATION #:			
DESCRIPTION (BREED/COLOR)			
COW'S SIRE		SIRE BREED:	
COW'S DAM		DAM BREED	
COW'S BIRTH DATE		WEANING WEIGHT	
PURCHASE DATE		PURCHASE PRICE	

BREEDING RECORD

WEIGHT AT FIRST SERVICE (KGS)				
AGE AT FIRST SERVICE (DAYS)				
HEAT DATES	DATE OF A.I/BULL SERVICE	PREG. DIAGNOSIS DATE	DATE TO DRY	DATE DUE TO CALF

COW ID

DATE OF SALE OR REMOVAL:	
REASON	
SALE WEIGHT	
SALE PRICE/LB.	
TOTAL VALUE	

	AGE AT FIRST CALVING (DAYS)			
	AGE AT CONCEPTION (DAYS)			
DATE CALVED	CALF SEX	CALF NO.	CALVING INTERNAL (DAYS)	NOTES

COW PRODUCTION HISTORY CARD

COW REGISTRATION #:			
DESCRIPTION (BREED/COLOR)			
COW'S SIRE		SIRE BREED:	
COW'S DAM		DAM BREED	
COW'S BIRTH DATE		WEANING WEIGHT	
PURCHASE DATE		PURCHASE PRICE	

BREEDING RECORD

WEIGHT AT FIRST SERVICE (KGS)			
AGE AT FIRST SERVICE (DAYS)			

HEAT DATES	DATE OF A.I/BULL SERVICE	PREG. DIAGNOSIS DATE	DATE TO DRY	DATE DUE TO CALF

COW ID

DATE OF SALE OR REMOVAL:	
REASON	
SALE WEIGHT	
SALE PRICE/LB.	
TOTAL VALUE	

AGE AT FIRST CALVING (DAYS)				
AGE AT CONCEPTION (DAYS)				
DATE CALVED	CALF SEX	CALF NO.	CALVING INTERNAL (DAYS)	NOTES

COW PRODUCTION HISTORY CARD

COW REGISTRATION #:			
DESCRIPTION (BREED/COLOR)			
COW'S SIRE		**SIRE BREED:**	
COW'S DAM		**DAM BREED**	
COW'S BIRTH DATE		**WEANING WEIGHT**	
PURCHASE DATE		**PURCHASE PRICE**	

BREEDING RECORD

WEIGHT AT FIRST SERVICE (KGS)				
AGE AT FIRST SERVICE (DAYS)				
HEAT DATES	**DATE OF A.I/BULL SERVICE**	**PREG. DIAGNOSIS DATE**	**DATE TO DRY**	**DATE DUE TO CALF**

COW ID #	

ATE OF SALE OR REMOVAL:	
REASON	
SALE WEIGHT	
SALE PRICE/LB.	
TOTAL VALUE	

	AGE AT FIRST CALVING (DAYS)			
	AGE AT CONCEPTION (DAYS)			
DATE CALVED	CALF SEX	CALF NO.	CALVING INTERNAL (DAYS)	NOTES

COW PRODUCTION HISTORY CARD

COW REGISTRATION #:

DESCRIPTION (BREED/COLOR)

COW'S SIRE		SIRE BREED:	
COW'S DAM		DAM BREED	
COW'S BIRTH DATE		WEANING WEIGHT	
PURCHASE DATE		PURCHASE PRICE	

BREEDING RECORD

WEIGHT AT FIRST SERVICE (KGS)			
AGE AT FIRST SERVICE (DAYS)			
HEAT DATES	DATE OF A.I/BULL SERVICE	PREG. DIAGNOSIS DATE	DATE TO DRY	DATE DUE TO CALF

COW ID

DATE OF SALE OR REMOVAL:	
REASON	
SALE WEIGHT	
SALE PRICE/LB.	
TOTAL VALUE	

	AGE AT FIRST CALVING (DAYS)			
	AGE AT CONCEPTION (DAYS)			
DATE CALVED	CALF SEX	CALF NO.	CALVING INTERNAL (DAYS)	NOTES

COW PRODUCTION HISTORY CARD

COW REGISTRATION #:			
DESCRIPTION (BREED/COLOR)			
COW'S SIRE		SIRE BREED:	
COW'S DAM		DAM BREED	
COW'S BIRTH DATE		WEANING WEIGHT	
PURCHASE DATE		PURCHASE PRICE	

BREEDING RECORD

WEIGHT AT FIRST SERVICE (KGS)				
AGE AT FIRST SERVICE (DAYS)				
HEAT DATES	DATE OF A.I/BULL SERVICE	PREG. DIAGNOSIS DATE	DATE TO DRY	DATE DUE TO CALF

COW ID #	

ATE OF SALE OR REMOVAL:	
REASON	
SALE WEIGHT	
SALE PRICE/LB.	
TOTAL VALUE	

AGE AT FIRST CALVING (DAYS)				
AGE AT CONCEPTION (DAYS)				
DATE CALVED	CALF SEX	CALF NO.	CALVING INTERNAL (DAYS)	NOTES

COW PRODUCTION HISTORY CARD

COW REGISTRATION #:			
DESCRIPTION (BREED/COLOR)			
COW'S SIRE		SIRE BREED:	
COW'S DAM		DAM BREED	
COW'S BIRTH DATE		WEANING WEIGHT	
PURCHASE DATE		PURCHASE PRICE	

BREEDING RECORD

WEIGHT AT FIRST SERVICE (KGS)				
AGE AT FIRST SERVICE (DAYS)				
HEAT DATES	DATE OF A.I/BULL SERVICE	PREG. DIAGNOSIS DATE	DATE TO DRY	DATE DUE TO CALF

COW ID #	

DATE OF SALE OR REMOVAL:	
REASON	
SALE WEIGHT	
SALE PRICE/LB.	
TOTAL VALUE	

AGE AT FIRST CALVING (DAYS)				
AGE AT CONCEPTION (DAYS)				
DATE CALVED	CALF SEX	CALF NO.	CALVING INTERNAL (DAYS)	NOTES

COW PRODUCTION HISTORY CARD

COW REGISTRATION #:			
DESCRIPTION (BREED/COLOR)			
COW'S SIRE		SIRE BREED:	
COW'S DAM		DAM BREED	
COW'S BIRTH DATE		WEANING WEIGHT	
PURCHASE DATE		PURCHASE PRICE	

BREEDING RECORD

WEIGHT AT FIRST SERVICE (KGS)			
AGE AT FIRST SERVICE (DAYS)			

HEAT DATES	DATE OF A.I/BULL SERVICE	PREG. DIAGNOSIS DATE	DATE TO DRY	DATE DUE TO CALF

COW ID #	

ATE OF SALE OR REMOVAL:	
REASON	
SALE WEIGHT	
SALE PRICE/LB.	
TOTAL VALUE	

AGE AT FIRST CALVING (DAYS)				
AGE AT CONCEPTION (DAYS)				
DATE CALVED	CALF SEX	CALF NO.	CALVING INTERNAL (DAYS)	NOTES

COW PRODUCTION HISTORY CARD

COW REGISTRATION #:			
DESCRIPTION (BREED/COLOR)			
COW'S SIRE		SIRE BREED:	
COW'S DAM		DAM BREED	
COW'S BIRTH DATE		WEANING WEIGHT	
PURCHASE DATE		PURCHASE PRICE	

BREEDING RECORD

WEIGHT AT FIRST SERVICE (KGS)				
AGE AT FIRST SERVICE (DAYS)				
HEAT DATES	DATE OF A.I/BULL SERVICE	PREG. DIAGNOSIS DATE	DATE TO DRY	DATE DUE TO CALF

COW ID #	

DATE OF SALE OR REMOVAL:	
REASON	
SALE WEIGHT	
SALE PRICE/LB.	
TOTAL VALUE	

	AGE AT FIRST CALVING (DAYS)			
	AGE AT CONCEPTION (DAYS)			
DATE CALVED	CALF SEX	CALF NO.	CALVING INTERNAL (DAYS)	NOTES

COW PRODUCTION HISTORY CARD

COW REGISTRATION #:			
DESCRIPTION (BREED/COLOR)			
COW'S SIRE		SIRE BREED:	
COW'S DAM		DAM BREED	
COW'S BIRTH DATE		WEANING WEIGHT	
PURCHASE DATE		PURCHASE PRICE	

BREEDING RECORD

WEIGHT AT FIRST SERVICE (KGS)				
AGE AT FIRST SERVICE (DAYS)				
HEAT DATES	DATE OF A.I/BULL SERVICE	PREG. DIAGNOSIS DATE	DATE TO DRY	DATE DUE TO CALF

COW ID #	

ATE OF SALE OR REMOVAL:	
REASON	
SALE WEIGHT	
SALE PRICE/LB.	
TOTAL VALUE	

AGE AT FIRST CALVING (DAYS)				
AGE AT CONCEPTION (DAYS)				
DATE CALVED	CALF SEX	CALF NO.	CALVING INTERNAL (DAYS)	NOTES

COW PRODUCTION HISTORY CARD

COW REGISTRATION #:			
DESCRIPTION (BREED/COLOR)			
COW'S SIRE		SIRE BREED:	
COW'S DAM		DAM BREED	
COW'S BIRTH DATE		WEANING WEIGHT	
PURCHASE DATE		PURCHASE PRICE	

BREEDING RECORD

WEIGHT AT FIRST SERVICE (KGS)				
AGE AT FIRST SERVICE (DAYS)				
HEAT DATES	DATE OF A.I/BULL SERVICE	PREG. DIAGNOSIS DATE	DATE TO DRY	DATE DUE TO CALF

COW ID

DATE OF SALE OR REMOVAL:	
REASON	
SALE WEIGHT	
SALE PRICE/LB.	
TOTAL VALUE	

AGE AT FIRST CALVING (DAYS)				
AGE AT CONCEPTION (DAYS)				
DATE CALVED	CALF SEX	CALF NO.	CALVING INTERNAL (DAYS)	NOTES

COW PRODUCTION HISTORY CARD

COW REGISTRATION #:			
DESCRIPTION (BREED/COLOR)			
COW'S SIRE		SIRE BREED:	
COW'S DAM		DAM BREED	
COW'S BIRTH DATE		WEANING WEIGHT	
PURCHASE DATE		PURCHASE PRICE	

BREEDING RECORD

	WEIGHT AT FIRST SERVICE (KGS)			
	AGE AT FIRST SERVICE (DAYS)			
HEAT DATES	DATE OF A.I/BULL SERVICE	PREG. DIAGNOSIS DATE	DATE TO DRY	DATE DUE TO CALF

COW ID

ATE OF SALE OR REMOVAL:	
REASON	
SALE WEIGHT	
SALE PRICE/LB.	
TOTAL VALUE	

	AGE AT FIRST CALVING (DAYS)				
	AGE AT CONCEPTION (DAYS)				
DATE CALVED	CALF SEX	CALF NO.	CALVING INTERNAL (DAYS)	NOTES	

COW PRODUCTION HISTORY CARD

COW REGISTRATION #:			
DESCRIPTION (BREED/COLOR)			
COW'S SIRE		SIRE BREED:	
COW'S DAM		DAM BREED	
COW'S BIRTH DATE		WEANING WEIGHT	
PURCHASE DATE		PURCHASE PRICE	

BREEDING RECORD

WEIGHT AT FIRST SERVICE (KGS)			
AGE AT FIRST SERVICE (DAYS)			

HEAT DATES	DATE OF A.I/BULL SERVICE	PREG. DIAGNOSIS DATE	DATE TO DRY	DATE DUE TO CALF

COW ID #	

DATE OF SALE OR REMOVAL:	
REASON	
SALE WEIGHT	
SALE PRICE/LB.	
TOTAL VALUE	

AGE AT FIRST CALVING (DAYS)				
AGE AT CONCEPTION (DAYS)				
DATE CALVED	CALF SEX	CALF NO.	CALVING INTERNAL (DAYS)	NOTES

COW PRODUCTION HISTORY CARD

COW REGISTRATION #:			
DESCRIPTION (BREED/COLOR)			
COW'S SIRE		SIRE BREED:	
COW'S DAM		DAM BREED	
COW'S BIRTH DATE		WEANING WEIGHT	
PURCHASE DATE		PURCHASE PRICE	

BREEDING RECORD

WEIGHT AT FIRST SERVICE (KGS)				
AGE AT FIRST SERVICE (DAYS)				
HEAT DATES	DATE OF A.I/BULL SERVICE	PREG. DIAGNOSIS DATE	DATE TO DRY	DATE DUE TO CALF

COW ID

DATE OF SALE OR REMOVAL:	
REASON	
SALE WEIGHT	
SALE PRICE/LB.	
TOTAL VALUE	

	AGE AT FIRST CALVING (DAYS)			
	AGE AT CONCEPTION (DAYS)			
DATE CALVED	CALF SEX	CALF NO.	CALVING INTERNAL (DAYS)	NOTES

COW PRODUCTION HISTORY CARD

COW REGISTRATION #:			
DESCRIPTION (BREED/COLOR)			
COW'S SIRE		SIRE BREED:	
COW'S DAM		DAM BREED	
COW'S BIRTH DATE		WEANING WEIGHT	
PURCHASE DATE		PURCHASE PRICE	

BREEDING RECORD

WEIGHT AT FIRST SERVICE (KGS)				
AGE AT FIRST SERVICE (DAYS)				
HEAT DATES	DATE OF A.I/BULL SERVICE	PREG. DIAGNOSIS DATE	DATE TO DRY	DATE DUE TO CALF

COW ID #	

DATE OF SALE OR REMOVAL:	
REASON	
SALE WEIGHT	
SALE PRICE/LB.	
TOTAL VALUE	

	AGE AT FIRST CALVING (DAYS)			
	AGE AT CONCEPTION (DAYS)			
DATE CALVED	CALF SEX	CALF NO.	CALVING INTERNAL (DAYS)	NOTES

COW PRODUCTION HISTORY CARD

COW REGISTRATION #:				
DESCRIPTION (BREED/COLOR)				
COW'S SIRE		SIRE BREED:		
COW'S DAM		DAM BREED		
COW'S BIRTH DATE		WEANING WEIGHT		
PURCHASE DATE		PURCHASE PRICE		

BREEDING RECORD

WEIGHT AT FIRST SERVICE (KGS)				
AGE AT FIRST SERVICE (DAYS)				
HEAT DATES	DATE OF A.I/BULL SERVICE	PREG. DIAGNOSIS DATE	DATE TO DRY	DATE DUE TO CALF

COW ID #	

ATE OF SALE OR REMOVAL:	
REASON	
SALE WEIGHT	
SALE PRICE/LB.	
TOTAL VALUE	

	AGE AT FIRST CALVING (DAYS)			
	AGE AT CONCEPTION (DAYS)			
DATE CALVED	CALF SEX	CALF NO.	CALVING INTERNAL (DAYS)	NOTES

COW PRODUCTION HISTORY CARD

COW REGISTRATION #:			
DESCRIPTION (BREED/COLOR)			
COW'S SIRE		SIRE BREED:	
COW'S DAM		DAM BREED	
COW'S BIRTH DATE		WEANING WEIGHT	
PURCHASE DATE		PURCHASE PRICE	

BREEDING RECORD

WEIGHT AT FIRST SERVICE (KGS)				
AGE AT FIRST SERVICE (DAYS)				
HEAT DATES	DATE OF A.I/BULL SERVICE	PREG. DIAGNOSIS DATE	DATE TO DRY	DATE DUE TO CALF

COW ID

DATE OF SALE OR REMOVAL:	
REASON	
SALE WEIGHT	
SALE PRICE/LB.	
TOTAL VALUE	

AGE AT FIRST CALVING (DAYS)				
AGE AT CONCEPTION (DAYS)				
DATE CALVED	CALF SEX	CALF NO.	CALVING INTERNAL (DAYS)	NOTES

COW PRODUCTION HISTORY CARD

COW REGISTRATION #:			

DESCRIPTION (BREED/COLOR)			

COW'S SIRE		SIRE BREED:	
COW'S DAM		DAM BREED	
COW'S BIRTH DATE		WEANING WEIGHT	
PURCHASE DATE		PURCHASE PRICE	

BREEDING RECORD

WEIGHT AT FIRST SERVICE (KGS)				
AGE AT FIRST SERVICE (DAYS)				
HEAT DATES	DATE OF A.I/BULL SERVICE	PREG. DIAGNOSIS DATE	DATE TO DRY	DATE DUE TO CALF

COW ID #	

ATE OF SALE OR REMOVAL:	
REASON	
SALE WEIGHT	
SALE PRICE/LB.	
TOTAL VALUE	

	AGE AT FIRST CALVING (DAYS)			
	AGE AT CONCEPTION (DAYS)			
DATE CALVED	CALF SEX	CALF NO.	CALVING INTERNAL (DAYS)	NOTES

COW PRODUCTION HISTORY CARD

COW REGISTRATION #:			
DESCRIPTION (BREED/COLOR)			
COW'S SIRE		SIRE BREED:	
COW'S DAM		DAM BREED	
COW'S BIRTH DATE		WEANING WEIGHT	
PURCHASE DATE		PURCHASE PRICE	

BREEDING RECORD

WEIGHT AT FIRST SERVICE (KGS)				
AGE AT FIRST SERVICE (DAYS)				
HEAT DATES	DATE OF A.I/BULL SERVICE	PREG. DIAGNOSIS DATE	DATE TO DRY	DATE DUE TO CALF

COW ID

DATE OF SALE OR REMOVAL:	
REASON	
SALE WEIGHT	
SALE PRICE/LB.	
TOTAL VALUE	

AGE AT FIRST CALVING (DAYS)				
AGE AT CONCEPTION (DAYS)				
DATE CALVED	CALF SEX	CALF NO.	CALVING INTERNAL (DAYS)	NOTES

COW PRODUCTION HISTORY CARD

COW REGISTRATION #:			
DESCRIPTION (BREED/COLOR)			
COW'S SIRE		SIRE BREED:	
COW'S DAM		DAM BREED	
COW'S BIRTH DATE		WEANING WEIGHT	
PURCHASE DATE		PURCHASE PRICE	

BREEDING RECORD

WEIGHT AT FIRST SERVICE (KGS)				
AGE AT FIRST SERVICE (DAYS)				
HEAT DATES	DATE OF A.I/BULL SERVICE	PREG. DIAGNOSIS DATE	DATE TO DRY	DATE DUE TO CALF

COW ID #	

ATE OF SALE OR REMOVAL:	
REASON	
SALE WEIGHT	
SALE PRICE/LB.	
TOTAL VALUE	

	AGE AT FIRST CALVING (DAYS)			
	AGE AT CONCEPTION (DAYS)			
DATE CALVED	CALF SEX	CALF NO.	CALVING INTERNAL (DAYS)	NOTES

COW PRODUCTION HISTORY CARD

COW REGISTRATION #:			
DESCRIPTION (BREED/COLOR)			
COW'S SIRE		SIRE BREED:	
COW'S DAM		DAM BREED	
COW'S BIRTH DATE		WEANING WEIGHT	
PURCHASE DATE		PURCHASE PRICE	

BREEDING RECORD

WEIGHT AT FIRST SERVICE (KGS)			
AGE AT FIRST SERVICE (DAYS)			

HEAT DATES	DATE OF A.I/BULL SERVICE	PREG. DIAGNOSIS DATE	DATE TO DRY	DATE DUE TO CALF

COW ID

DATE OF SALE OR REMOVAL:	
REASON	
SALE WEIGHT	
SALE PRICE/LB.	
TOTAL VALUE	

AGE AT FIRST CALVING (DAYS)				
AGE AT CONCEPTION (DAYS)				
DATE CALVED	CALF SEX	CALF NO.	CALVING INTERNAL (DAYS)	NOTES

COW PRODUCTION HISTORY CARD

COW REGISTRATION #:			
DESCRIPTION (BREED/COLOR)			
COW'S SIRE		SIRE BREED:	
COW'S DAM		DAM BREED	
COW'S BIRTH DATE		WEANING WEIGHT	
PURCHASE DATE		PURCHASE PRICE	

BREEDING RECORD

	WEIGHT AT FIRST SERVICE (KGS)			
	AGE AT FIRST SERVICE (DAYS)			
HEAT DATES	DATE OF A.I/BULL SERVICE	PREG. DIAGNOSIS DATE	DATE TO DRY	DATE DUE TO CALF

COW ID #	

ATE OF SALE OR REMOVAL:	
REASON	
SALE WEIGHT	
SALE PRICE/LB.	
TOTAL VALUE	

	AGE AT FIRST CALVING (DAYS)			
	AGE AT CONCEPTION (DAYS)			
DATE CALVED	CALF SEX	CALF NO.	CALVING INTERNAL (DAYS)	NOTES

COW PRODUCTION HISTORY CARD

COW REGISTRATION #:			
DESCRIPTION (BREED/COLOR)			
COW'S SIRE		SIRE BREED:	
COW'S DAM		DAM BREED	
COW'S BIRTH DATE		WEANING WEIGHT	
PURCHASE DATE		PURCHASE PRICE	

BREEDING RECORD

WEIGHT AT FIRST SERVICE (KGS)				
AGE AT FIRST SERVICE (DAYS)				
HEAT DATES	DATE OF A.I/BULL SERVICE	PREG. DIAGNOSIS DATE	DATE TO DRY	DATE DUE TO CALF

COW ID

DATE OF SALE OR REMOVAL:	
REASON	
SALE WEIGHT	
SALE PRICE/LB.	
TOTAL VALUE	

AGE AT FIRST CALVING (DAYS)				
AGE AT CONCEPTION (DAYS)				
DATE CALVED	CALF SEX	CALF NO.	CALVING INTERNAL (DAYS)	NOTES

COW PRODUCTION HISTORY CARD

COW REGISTRATION #:				
DESCRIPTION (BREED/COLOR)				
COW'S SIRE		SIRE BREED:		
COW'S DAM		DAM BREED		
COW'S BIRTH DATE		WEANING WEIGHT		
PURCHASE DATE		PURCHASE PRICE		

BREEDING RECORD

	WEIGHT AT FIRST SERVICE (KGS)			
	AGE AT FIRST SERVICE (DAYS)			
HEAT DATES	DATE OF A.I/BULL SERVICE	PREG. DIAGNOSIS DATE	DATE TO DRY	DATE DUE TO CALF

COW ID #	

ATE OF SALE OR REMOVAL:	
REASON	
SALE WEIGHT	
SALE PRICE/LB.	
TOTAL VALUE	

	AGE AT FIRST CALVING (DAYS)			
	AGE AT CONCEPTION (DAYS)			
DATE CALVED	CALF SEX	CALF NO.	CALVING INTERNAL (DAYS)	NOTES

COW PRODUCTION HISTORY CARD

COW REGISTRATION #:			
DESCRIPTION (BREED/COLOR)			
COW'S SIRE		SIRE BREED:	
COW'S DAM		DAM BREED	
COW'S BIRTH DATE		WEANING WEIGHT	
PURCHASE DATE		PURCHASE PRICE	

BREEDING RECORD

WEIGHT AT FIRST SERVICE (KGS)				
AGE AT FIRST SERVICE (DAYS)				
HEAT DATES	DATE OF A.I/BULL SERVICE	PREG. DIAGNOSIS DATE	DATE TO DRY	DATE DUE TO CALF

COW ID #	

DATE OF SALE OR REMOVAL:	
REASON	
SALE WEIGHT	
SALE PRICE/LB.	
TOTAL VALUE	

	AGE AT FIRST CALVING (DAYS)			
	AGE AT CONCEPTION (DAYS)			
DATE CALVED	CALF SEX	CALF NO.	CALVING INTERNAL (DAYS)	NOTES

COW PRODUCTION HISTORY CARD

COW REGISTRATION #:			
DESCRIPTION (BREED/COLOR)			
COW'S SIRE		SIRE BREED:	
COW'S DAM		DAM BREED	
COW'S BIRTH DATE		WEANING WEIGHT	
PURCHASE DATE		PURCHASE PRICE	

BREEDING RECORD

WEIGHT AT FIRST SERVICE (KGS)				
AGE AT FIRST SERVICE (DAYS)				
HEAT DATES	DATE OF A.I/BULL SERVICE	PREG. DIAGNOSIS DATE	DATE TO DRY	DATE DUE TO CALF

COW ID #	

ATE OF SALE OR REMOVAL:	
REASON	
SALE WEIGHT	
SALE PRICE/LB.	
TOTAL VALUE	

AGE AT FIRST CALVING (DAYS)				
AGE AT CONCEPTION (DAYS)				
DATE CALVED	CALF SEX	CALF NO.	CALVING INTERNAL (DAYS)	NOTES

COW PRODUCTION HISTORY CARD

COW REGISTRATION #:

DESCRIPTION (BREED/COLOR)

COW'S SIRE		SIRE BREED:	
COW'S DAM		DAM BREED	
COW'S BIRTH DATE		WEANING WEIGHT	
PURCHASE DATE		PURCHASE PRICE	

BREEDING RECORD

WEIGHT AT FIRST SERVICE (KGS)			
AGE AT FIRST SERVICE (DAYS)			
HEAT DATES	DATE OF A.I/BULL SERVICE	PREG. DIAGNOSIS DATE	DATE TO DRY	DATE DUE TO CALF

COW ID

DATE OF SALE OR REMOVAL:	
REASON	
SALE WEIGHT	
SALE PRICE/LB.	
TOTAL VALUE	

AGE AT FIRST CALVING (DAYS)				
AGE AT CONCEPTION (DAYS)				
DATE CALVED	CALF SEX	CALF NO.	CALVING INTERNAL (DAYS)	NOTES

COW PRODUCTION HISTORY CARD

COW REGISTRATION #:			
DESCRIPTION (BREED/COLOR)			
COW'S SIRE		SIRE BREED:	
COW'S DAM		DAM BREED	
COW'S BIRTH DATE		WEANING WEIGHT	
PURCHASE DATE		PURCHASE PRICE	

BREEDING RECORD

WEIGHT AT FIRST SERVICE (KGS)				
AGE AT FIRST SERVICE (DAYS)				
HEAT DATES	DATE OF A.I/BULL SERVICE	PREG. DIAGNOSIS DATE	DATE TO DRY	DATE DUE TO CALF

COW ID

ATE OF SALE OR REMOVAL:	
REASON	
SALE WEIGHT	
SALE PRICE/LB.	
TOTAL VALUE	

AGE AT FIRST CALVING (DAYS)				
AGE AT CONCEPTION (DAYS)				
DATE CALVED	CALF SEX	CALF NO.	CALVING INTERNAL (DAYS)	NOTES

COW PRODUCTION HISTORY CARD

COW REGISTRATION #:			
DESCRIPTION (BREED/COLOR)			
COW'S SIRE		SIRE BREED:	
COW'S DAM		DAM BREED	
COW'S BIRTH DATE		WEANING WEIGHT	
PURCHASE DATE		PURCHASE PRICE	

BREEDING RECORD

WEIGHT AT FIRST SERVICE (KGS)			
AGE AT FIRST SERVICE (DAYS)			

HEAT DATES	DATE OF A.I/BULL SERVICE	PREG. DIAGNOSIS DATE	DATE TO DRY	DATE DUE TO CALF

COW ID

DATE OF SALE OR REMOVAL:	
REASON	
SALE WEIGHT	
SALE PRICE/LB.	
TOTAL VALUE	

AGE AT FIRST CALVING (DAYS)				
AGE AT CONCEPTION (DAYS)				
DATE CALVED	CALF SEX	CALF NO.	CALVING INTERNAL (DAYS)	NOTES

COW PRODUCTION HISTORY CARD

COW REGISTRATION #:			
DESCRIPTION (BREED/COLOR)			
COW'S SIRE		SIRE BREED:	
COW'S DAM		DAM BREED	
COW'S BIRTH DATE		WEANING WEIGHT	
PURCHASE DATE		PURCHASE PRICE	

BREEDING RECORD

WEIGHT AT FIRST SERVICE (KGS)				
AGE AT FIRST SERVICE (DAYS)				
HEAT DATES	DATE OF A.I/BULL SERVICE	PREG. DIAGNOSIS DATE	DATE TO DRY	DATE DUE TO CALF

COW ID #	

ATE OF SALE OR REMOVAL:	
REASON	
SALE WEIGHT	
SALE PRICE/LB.	
TOTAL VALUE	

	AGE AT FIRST CALVING (DAYS)			
	AGE AT CONCEPTION (DAYS)			
ATE CALVED	CALF SEX	CALF NO.	CALVING INTERNAL (DAYS)	NOTES

COW PRODUCTION HISTORY CARD

COW REGISTRATION #:			
DESCRIPTION (BREED/COLOR)			
COW'S SIRE		SIRE BREED:	
COW'S DAM		DAM BREED	
COW'S BIRTH DATE		WEANING WEIGHT	
PURCHASE DATE		PURCHASE PRICE	

BREEDING RECORD

WEIGHT AT FIRST SERVICE (KGS)				
AGE AT FIRST SERVICE (DAYS)				
HEAT DATES	DATE OF A.I/BULL SERVICE	PREG. DIAGNOSIS DATE	DATE TO DRY	DATE DUE TO CALF

COW ID

DATE OF SALE OR REMOVAL:	
REASON	
SALE WEIGHT	
SALE PRICE/LB.	
TOTAL VALUE	

AGE AT FIRST CALVING (DAYS)				
AGE AT CONCEPTION (DAYS)				
DATE CALVED	CALF SEX	CALF NO.	CALVING INTERNAL (DAYS)	NOTES

COW PRODUCTION HISTORY CARD

COW REGISTRATION #:			
DESCRIPTION (BREED/COLOR)			
COW'S SIRE		SIRE BREED:	
COW'S DAM		DAM BREED	
COW'S BIRTH DATE		WEANING WEIGHT	
PURCHASE DATE		PURCHASE PRICE	

BREEDING RECORD

WEIGHT AT FIRST SERVICE (KGS)				
AGE AT FIRST SERVICE (DAYS)				
HEAT DATES	DATE OF A.I/BULL SERVICE	PREG. DIAGNOSIS DATE	DATE TO DRY	DATE DUE TO CALF

COW ID #	

DATE OF SALE OR REMOVAL:	
REASON	
SALE WEIGHT	
SALE PRICE/LB.	
TOTAL VALUE	

	AGE AT FIRST CALVING (DAYS)			
	AGE AT CONCEPTION (DAYS)			
DATE CALVED	CALF SEX	CALF NO.	CALVING INTERNAL (DAYS)	NOTES

COW PRODUCTION HISTORY CARD

COW REGISTRATION #:			
DESCRIPTION (BREED/COLOR)			
COW'S SIRE		SIRE BREED:	
COW'S DAM		DAM BREED	
COW'S BIRTH DATE		WEANING WEIGHT	
PURCHASE DATE		PURCHASE PRICE	

BREEDING RECORD

WEIGHT AT FIRST SERVICE (KGS)				
AGE AT FIRST SERVICE (DAYS)				
HEAT DATES	DATE OF A.I/BULL SERVICE	PREG. DIAGNOSIS DATE	DATE TO DRY	DATE DUE TO CALF

COW ID #	

DATE OF SALE OR REMOVAL:	
REASON	
SALE WEIGHT	
SALE PRICE/LB.	
TOTAL VALUE	

	AGE AT FIRST CALVING (DAYS)			
	AGE AT CONCEPTION (DAYS)			
DATE CALVED	CALF SEX	CALF NO.	CALVING INTERNAL (DAYS)	NOTES

COW PRODUCTION HISTORY CARD

COW REGISTRATION #:			
DESCRIPTION (BREED/COLOR)			
COW'S SIRE		**SIRE BREED:**	
COW'S DAM		**DAM BREED**	
COW'S BIRTH DATE		**WEANING WEIGHT**	
PURCHASE DATE		**PURCHASE PRICE**	

BREEDING RECORD

WEIGHT AT FIRST SERVICE (KGS)				
AGE AT FIRST SERVICE (DAYS)				
HEAT DATES	DATE OF A.I/BULL SERVICE	PREG. DIAGNOSIS DATE	DATE TO DRY	DATE DUE TO CALF

COW ID #	

ATE OF SALE OR REMOVAL:	
REASON	
SALE WEIGHT	
SALE PRICE/LB.	
TOTAL VALUE	

	AGE AT FIRST CALVING (DAYS)				
	AGE AT CONCEPTION (DAYS)				
DATE CALVED	CALF SEX	CALF NO.	CALVING INTERNAL (DAYS)	NOTES	

COW PRODUCTION HISTORY CARD

COW REGISTRATION #:			
DESCRIPTION (BREED/COLOR)			
COW'S SIRE		SIRE BREED:	
COW'S DAM		DAM BREED	
COW'S BIRTH DATE		WEANING WEIGHT	
PURCHASE DATE		PURCHASE PRICE	

BREEDING RECORD

	WEIGHT AT FIRST SERVICE (KGS)			
	AGE AT FIRST SERVICE (DAYS)			
HEAT DATES	DATE OF A.I/BULL SERVICE	PREG. DIAGNOSIS DATE	DATE TO DRY	DATE DUE TO CALF

COW ID

DATE OF SALE OR REMOVAL:	
REASON	
SALE WEIGHT	
SALE PRICE/LB.	
TOTAL VALUE	

AGE AT FIRST CALVING (DAYS)				
AGE AT CONCEPTION (DAYS)				
DATE CALVED	CALF SEX	CALF NO.	CALVING INTERNAL (DAYS)	NOTES

COW PRODUCTION HISTORY CARD

COW REGISTRATION #:			
DESCRIPTION (BREED/COLOR)			
COW'S SIRE		SIRE BREED:	
COW'S DAM		DAM BREED	
COW'S BIRTH DATE		WEANING WEIGHT	
PURCHASE DATE		PURCHASE PRICE	

BREEDING RECORD

WEIGHT AT FIRST SERVICE (KGS)				
AGE AT FIRST SERVICE (DAYS)				
HEAT DATES	DATE OF A.I/BULL SERVICE	PREG. DIAGNOSIS DATE	DATE TO DRY	DATE DUE TO CALF

COW ID

ATE OF SALE OR REMOVAL:	
REASON	
SALE WEIGHT	
SALE PRICE/LB.	
TOTAL VALUE	

	AGE AT FIRST CALVING (DAYS)				
	AGE AT CONCEPTION (DAYS)				
ATE CALVED	CALF SEX	CALF NO.	CALVING INTERNAL (DAYS)	NOTES	

COW PRODUCTION HISTORY CARD

COW REGISTRATION #:			
DESCRIPTION (BREED/COLOR)			
COW'S SIRE		SIRE BREED:	
COW'S DAM		DAM BREED	
COW'S BIRTH DATE		WEANING WEIGHT	
PURCHASE DATE		PURCHASE PRICE	

BREEDING RECORD

WEIGHT AT FIRST SERVICE (KGS)				
AGE AT FIRST SERVICE (DAYS)				
HEAT DATES	DATE OF A.I/BULL SERVICE	PREG. DIAGNOSIS DATE	DATE TO DRY	DATE DUE TO CALF

COW ID

DATE OF SALE OR REMOVAL:	
REASON	
SALE WEIGHT	
SALE PRICE/LB.	
TOTAL VALUE	

	AGE AT FIRST CALVING (DAYS)			
	AGE AT CONCEPTION (DAYS)			
DATE CALVED	CALF SEX	CALF NO.	CALVING INTERNAL (DAYS)	NOTES

COW PRODUCTION HISTORY CARD

COW REGISTRATION #:			
DESCRIPTION (BREED/COLOR)			
COW'S SIRE		SIRE BREED:	
COW'S DAM		DAM BREED	
COW'S BIRTH DATE		WEANING WEIGHT	
PURCHASE DATE		PURCHASE PRICE	

BREEDING RECORD

WEIGHT AT FIRST SERVICE (KGS)				
AGE AT FIRST SERVICE (DAYS)				
HEAT DATES	DATE OF A.I/BULL SERVICE	PREG. DIAGNOSIS DATE	DATE TO DRY	DATE DUE TO CALF

COW ID

ATE OF SALE OR REMOVAL:	
REASON	
SALE WEIGHT	
SALE PRICE/LB.	
TOTAL VALUE	

	AGE AT FIRST CALVING (DAYS)				
	AGE AT CONCEPTION (DAYS)				
DATE CALVED	CALF SEX	CALF NO.	CALVING INTERNAL (DAYS)	NOTES	

COW PRODUCTION HISTORY CARD

COW REGISTRATION #:			
DESCRIPTION (BREED/COLOR)			
COW'S SIRE		SIRE BREED:	
COW'S DAM		DAM BREED	
COW'S BIRTH DATE		WEANING WEIGHT	
PURCHASE DATE		PURCHASE PRICE	

BREEDING RECORD

WEIGHT AT FIRST SERVICE (KGS)			
AGE AT FIRST SERVICE (DAYS)			

HEAT DATES	DATE OF A.I/BULL SERVICE	PREG. DIAGNOSIS DATE	DATE TO DRY	DATE DUE TO CALF

COW ID #	

DATE OF SALE OR REMOVAL:	
REASON	
SALE WEIGHT	
SALE PRICE/LB.	
TOTAL VALUE	

	AGE AT FIRST CALVING (DAYS)			
	AGE AT CONCEPTION (DAYS)			
DATE CALVED	CALF SEX	CALF NO.	CALVING INTERNAL (DAYS)	NOTES

COW PRODUCTION HISTORY CARD

COW REGISTRATION #:			
DESCRIPTION (BREED/COLOR)			
COW'S SIRE		SIRE BREED:	
COW'S DAM		DAM BREED	
COW'S BIRTH DATE		WEANING WEIGHT	
PURCHASE DATE		PURCHASE PRICE	

BREEDING RECORD

WEIGHT AT FIRST SERVICE (KGS)				
AGE AT FIRST SERVICE (DAYS)				
HEAT DATES	DATE OF A.I/BULL SERVICE	PREG. DIAGNOSIS DATE	DATE TO DRY	DATE DUE TO CALF

COW ID

ATE OF SALE OR REMOVAL:	
REASON	
SALE WEIGHT	
SALE PRICE/LB.	
TOTAL VALUE	

	AGE AT FIRST CALVING (DAYS)				
	AGE AT CONCEPTION (DAYS)				
DATE CALVED	CALF SEX	CALF NO.	CALVING INTERNAL (DAYS)	NOTES	

COW PRODUCTION HISTORY CARD

COW REGISTRATION #:			
DESCRIPTION (BREED/COLOR)			
COW'S SIRE		SIRE BREED:	
COW'S DAM		DAM BREED	
COW'S BIRTH DATE		WEANING WEIGHT	
PURCHASE DATE		PURCHASE PRICE	

BREEDING RECORD

	WEIGHT AT FIRST SERVICE (KGS)			
	AGE AT FIRST SERVICE (DAYS)			
HEAT DATES	DATE OF A.I/BULL SERVICE	PREG. DIAGNOSIS DATE	DATE TO DRY	DATE DUE T(CALF

COW ID

DATE OF SALE OR REMOVAL:	
REASON	
SALE WEIGHT	
SALE PRICE/LB.	
TOTAL VALUE	

	AGE AT FIRST CALVING (DAYS)			
	AGE AT CONCEPTION (DAYS)			
DATE CALVED	CALF SEX	CALF NO.	CALVING INTERNAL (DAYS)	NOTES

COW PRODUCTION HISTORY CARD

COW REGISTRATION #:			
DESCRIPTION (BREED/COLOR)			
COW'S SIRE		SIRE BREED:	
COW'S DAM		DAM BREED	
COW'S BIRTH DATE		WEANING WEIGHT	
PURCHASE DATE		PURCHASE PRICE	

BREEDING RECORD

WEIGHT AT FIRST SERVICE (KGS)			
AGE AT FIRST SERVICE (DAYS)			

HEAT DATES	DATE OF A.I/BULL SERVICE	PREG. DIAGNOSIS DATE	DATE TO DRY	DATE DUE TO CALF

COW ID #	

ATE OF SALE OR REMOVAL:	
REASON	
SALE WEIGHT	
SALE PRICE/LB.	
TOTAL VALUE	

	AGE AT FIRST CALVING (DAYS)				
	AGE AT CONCEPTION (DAYS)				
DATE CALVED	CALF SEX	CALF NO.	CALVING INTERNAL (DAYS)	NOTES	

COW PRODUCTION HISTORY CARD

COW REGISTRATION #:			
DESCRIPTION (BREED/COLOR)			
COW'S SIRE		SIRE BREED:	
COW'S DAM		DAM BREED	
COW'S BIRTH DATE		WEANING WEIGHT	
PURCHASE DATE		PURCHASE PRICE	

BREEDING RECORD

WEIGHT AT FIRST SERVICE (KGS)			
AGE AT FIRST SERVICE (DAYS)			

HEAT DATES	DATE OF A.I/BULL SERVICE	PREG. DIAGNOSIS DATE	DATE TO DRY	DATE DUE TO CALF

COW ID

DATE OF SALE OR REMOVAL:	
REASON	
SALE WEIGHT	
SALE PRICE/LB.	
TOTAL VALUE	

AGE AT FIRST CALVING (DAYS)				
AGE AT CONCEPTION (DAYS)				
DATE CALVED	CALF SEX	CALF NO.	CALVING INTERNAL (DAYS)	NOTES

COW PRODUCTION HISTORY CARD

COW REGISTRATION #:			
DESCRIPTION (BREED/COLOR)			
COW'S SIRE		SIRE BREED:	
COW'S DAM		DAM BREED	
COW'S BIRTH DATE		WEANING WEIGHT	
PURCHASE DATE		PURCHASE PRICE	

BREEDING RECORD

WEIGHT AT FIRST SERVICE (KGS)				
AGE AT FIRST SERVICE (DAYS)				
HEAT DATES	DATE OF A.I/BULL SERVICE	PREG. DIAGNOSIS DATE	DATE TO DRY	DATE DUE TO CALF

COW ID

ATE OF SALE OR REMOVAL:	
REASON	
SALE WEIGHT	
SALE PRICE/LB.	
TOTAL VALUE	

	AGE AT FIRST CALVING (DAYS)			
	AGE AT CONCEPTION (DAYS)			
DATE CALVED	CALF SEX	CALF NO.	CALVING INTERNAL (DAYS)	NOTES

MEDICAL LOG

DATE	COW ID	MEDICATION	DOSAGE	DIAGNOSIS	NOTES

DEWORMING & IMMUNIZATIONS

DATE	COW ID	TYPE	DOSAGE	DUE NEXT	NOTES

MEDICAL LOG

DATE	COW ID	MEDICATION	DOSAGE	DIAGNOSIS	NOTES

EWORMING & IMMUNIZATIONS

DATE	COW ID	TYPE	DOSAGE	DUE NEXT	NOTES

MEDICAL LOG

DATE	COW ID	MEDICATION	DOSAGE	DIAGNOSIS	NOTES

DEWORMING & IMMUNIZATIONS

DATE	COW ID	TYPE	DOSAGE	DUE NEXT	NOTES

MEDICAL LOG

DATE	COW ID	MEDICATION	DOSAGE	DIAGNOSIS	NOTES

EWORMING & IMMUNIZATIONS

DATE	COW ID	TYPE	DOSAGE	DUE NEXT	NOTES

CATTLE SALES RECORD

DATE	CLASS OF CATTLE	ID NUMBER	WEIGHT	PRICE PER POUND	TOTAL PRIC
TOTAL SALES					$

EXPENSE RECORDS

EXPENSE ITEM						
DATE	DESCRIPTION	FEED	SUPPLIES	MEDICAL	OTHER	TOTAL COST
TOTAL EXPENSES						$
NET PROFIT OR LOSS (TOTAL INCOME MINUS TOTAL EXPENSES)						$

CATTLE SALES RECORD

DATE	CLASS OF CATTLE	ID NUMBER	WEIGHT	PRICE PER POUND	TOTAL PRICE
TOTAL SALES					$

XPENSE RECORDS

DATE	DESCRIPTION	FEED	SUPPLIES	MEDICAL	OTHER	TOTAL COST
TAL EXPENSES						$
PROFIT OR LOSS (TOTAL INCOME MINUS TOTAL EXPENSES)						$

CATTLE SALES RECORD

DATE	CLASS OF CATTLE	ID NUMBER	WEIGHT	PRICE PER POUND	TOTAL PRIC
TOTAL SALES					$

EXPENSE RECORDS

EXPENSE ITEM						
DATE	DESCRIPTION	FEED	SUPPLIES	MEDICAL	OTHER	TOTAL COST
TOTAL EXPENSES						$
NET PROFIT OR LOSS (TOTAL INCOME MINUS TOTAL EXPENSES)						$

CATTLE SALES RECORD

DATE	CLASS OF CATTLE	ID NUMBER	WEIGHT	PRICE PER POUND	TOTAL PRICE
TOTAL SALES					$

XPENSE RECORDS

ENSE ITEM						
)ATE	DESCRIPTION	FEED	SUPPLIES	MEDICAL	OTHER	TOTAL COST
'AL EXPENSES						$
PROFIT OR LOSS (TOTAL INCOME MINUS TOTAL EXPENSES)						$

NOTES

NOTES

NOTES

NOTES

NOTES

NOTES

Made in the USA
Las Vegas, NV
06 October 2023

78675211R00083